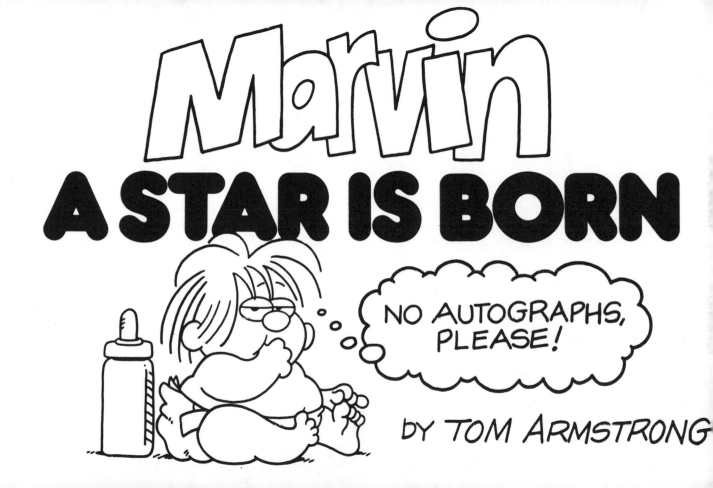

For Glenda, Jonathan, and Jennifer

Library of Congress Cataloging in Publication Data

Armstrong, Tom, 1950-
   Marvin.

   1. Infants—Caricatures and cartoons. 2. American wit and humor, Pictorial. I. Title.
NC1429.A639A4 1982   741.5'973   82-40388
ISBN 0-89480-237-2 (pbk.)

Workman Publishing Company, Inc.
1 West 39th Street
New York, N.Y. 10018

Manufactured in Untied States of America
First printing September 1982

10 9 8 7 6 5 4 3 2 1

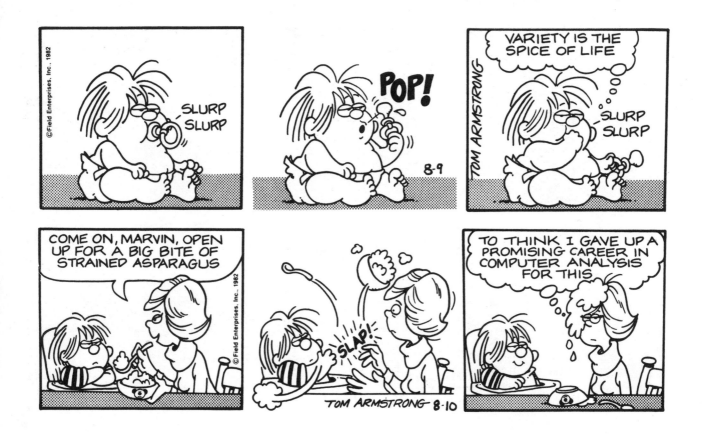

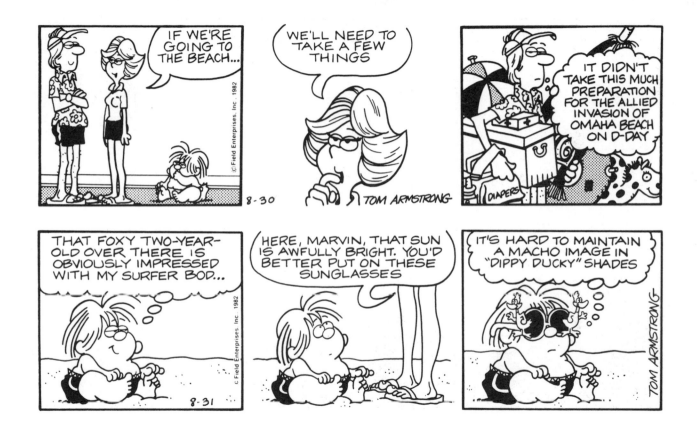

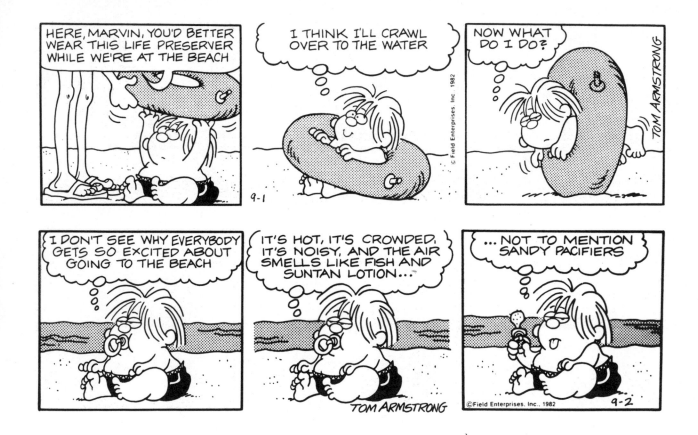

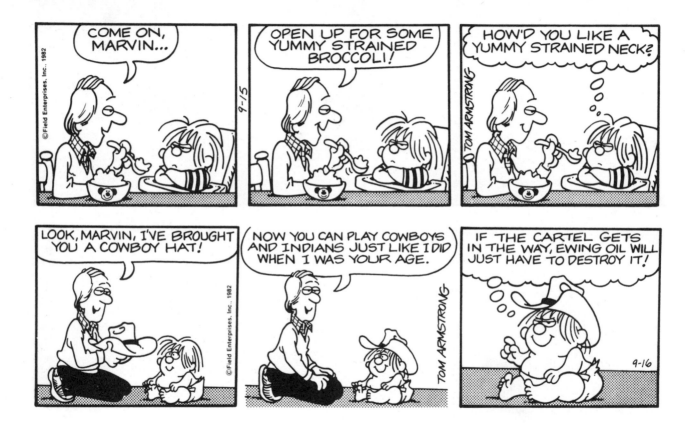

BABY'S FIRST PHOTOGRAPH

Already showing early signs of future stardom.

BABY'S FIRST SMILE

Right after sneezing while being fed by daddy.

BABY'S FIRST VISIT TO THE DOCTOR

Marvin came prepared for his immunizations.

BABY'S FIRST CARTRIP

It took 45 minutes and 3 diapers to go to the corner grocery store.

BABY'S FIRST HAIRCUT

Marvin didn't hold still!

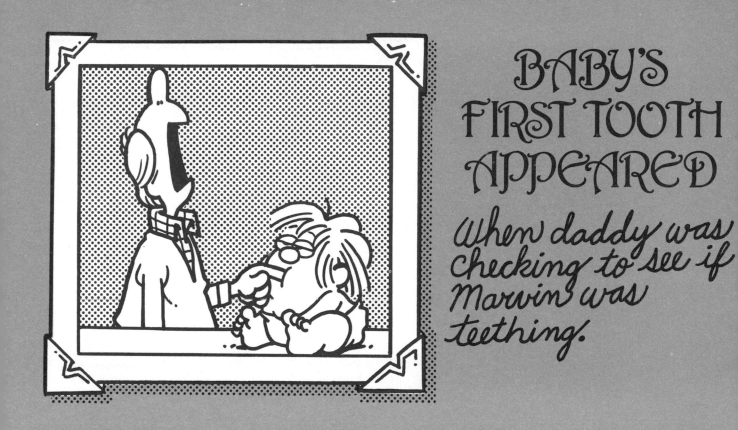

BABY'S FIRST TOOTH APPEARED

When daddy was checking to see if Marvin was teething.

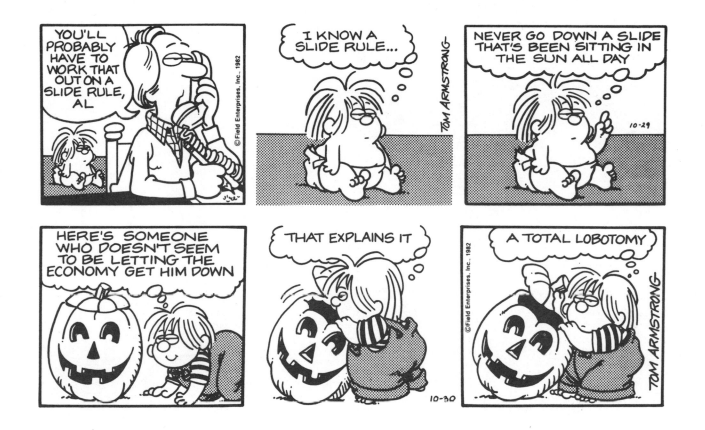

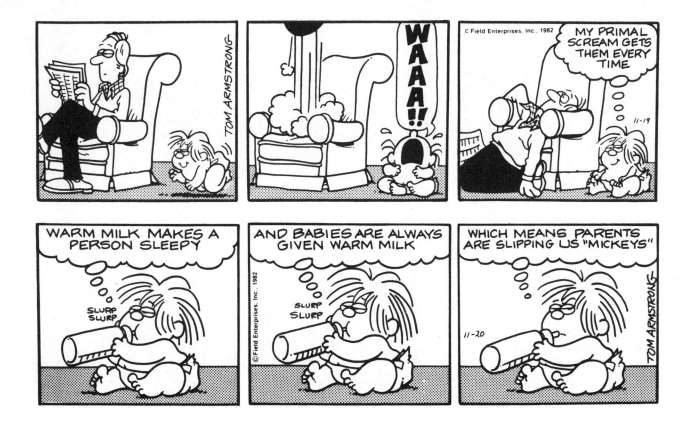